DINO RIDDLE

You can solve this riddle using the letters in the riddle itself. Just number the letters, left to right, from 1 to 26. Then, write the letters in the spaces with their numbers. We filled in the first one to get you started: "A" is the 3rd letter in the riddle, so it goes in the space marked "3rd."

What dinosaur is a good sleeper?

A _ _ _ _ _ - _ _ _ _ _ _ - _ _
3rd 9th 4th 22nd 16th 8th   14th 7th 8th 26th 23rd   11th 20th

Answer on page 33

TILE TOTALS

It is a busy day for Dan's Tile Toters. Dan's workers will be putting down new tiles on five different patios in town. Can you figure out how many tiles they will need for each job?

Illustration: Scott Peck

1

2

Hint on page 32

Answer on page 33

Remember, although some tiles may be hidden by trees and other objects, every patio is a rectangle.

Can you also figure out how many tiles Dan will need in all?

Here is the front page of the *Mathmania Gazette*. Some stories use exact numbers. Others are estimates—numbers that are close to the exact figures. Can you figure out which numbers are exact and which are estimates?

Mathmania Gazette

Woman Gives Birth to Triplets

Crowd of nearly 30,000 sees Reds beat Stingrays

Sunken Ship Treasure Valued at More than $1 Million

Heat Wave! Temperatures to Top 100°

Blue Sox Lose 10th in a Row!

Palmer City Man Celebrates 100th Birthday

Space Mission to last up to 6 Months

Illustration: Lindy Burnett

Answer on page 33

FOLLOW THE FLAKES

Can you find a path from START to FINISH that adds up to 21? You can move across, up, down or diagonally from one snowflake to the next.

START

FINISH

Answer on page 33

PIG GIGGLE

The collection of shapes is really a secret message. Crack the code and you will have the answer to the riddle at the bottom of the opposite page. Each shape is made from some of the squares and triangles in the number grid. When you find

Illustration: Jerry Zimmerman

a shape, add the numbers in its squares and triangles. (Do not turn the shapes.) Then find the blank that matches your sum for each shape and fill it in by writing the letter you see next to the shape.

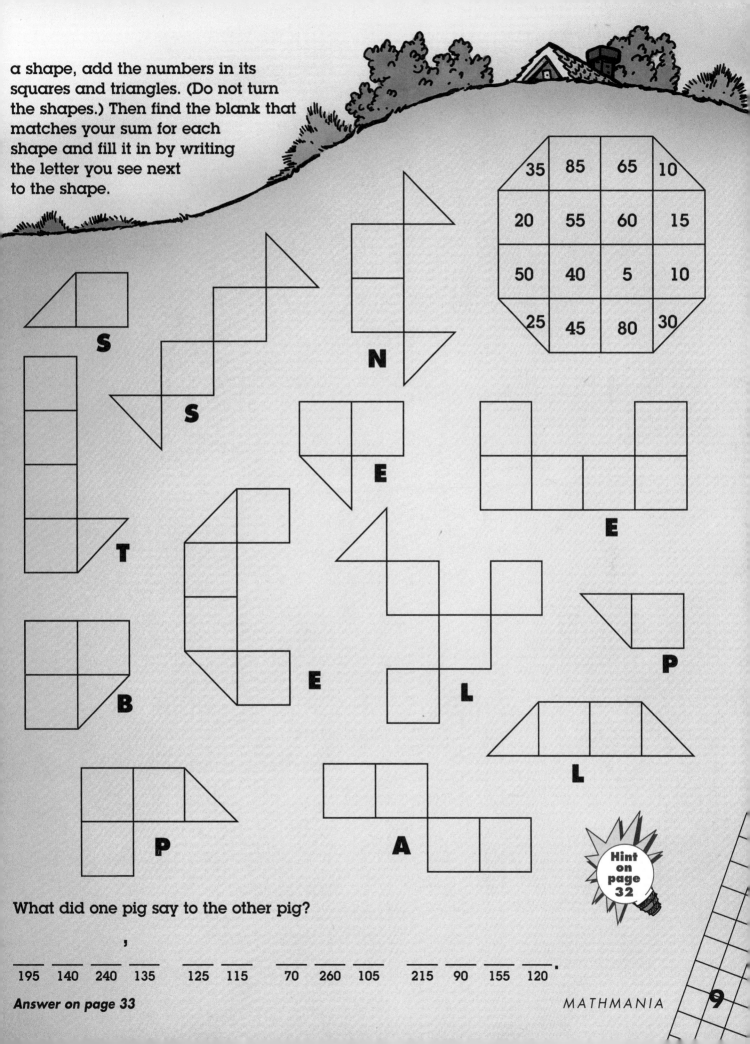

35	85	65	10
20	55	60	15
50	40	5	10
25	45	80	30

S

S

N

E

T

E

E

B

E

L

P

B

L

P

A

What did one pig say to the other pig?

$\overline{\rule{1em}{0.4pt}}\ \overline{\rule{1em}{0.4pt}}\ \overline{\rule{1em}{0.4pt}}\ \overline{\rule{1em}{0.4pt}}$, $\overline{\rule{1em}{0.4pt}}\ \overline{\rule{1em}{0.4pt}}$ $\overline{\rule{1em}{0.4pt}}\ \overline{\rule{1em}{0.4pt}}\ \overline{\rule{1em}{0.4pt}}$ $\overline{\rule{1em}{0.4pt}}\ \overline{\rule{1em}{0.4pt}}\ \overline{\rule{1em}{0.4pt}}$.

195 140 240 135   125 115   70 260 105   215 90 155 120

Hint on page 32

Answer on page 33

TRIANGLE TRAP

Charlotte has spun a wonderful web filled with triangles. Are there more than 50? Try counting this tangle of triangles to see for yourself.

Illustration: Terry Kovalcik

Answer on page 33

FRUZZLE PUZZLE

Hint on page 32

*T*hese are Fruzzles.

These are not Fruzzles.

Can you figure out which of these are Fruzzles?
Hint: The creatures need to have three things in common to be Fruzzles.

A

B

C

D

E

F

G

H

I

J

K

Answer on page 33

Three, six, nine, and you're doing fine. Try to connect the dots by counting by threes to come up with a well-known "three."

•24
•21
•27
•30 •33 •36
18•   •39
45•
•42
•48
•51 •57 •60
12• •15 •84
81• •54 •63
•6 93• •87 66•
9• •3 •132 •90 •78 •69
•102
105• •129 •72
•75
108• •126
99• •96
111• •123
114• 120•
117•

Illustration: Rob Sepanak

TABLE TROUBLE

Kendra is in charge of seating people at the annual Valentine's Dance. She must put the numbers 1 to 12 on the tables so that people with the matching tickets will know where to go. Unfortunately, she left her list at home. Can you help her finish the job? The total number on each of the six sides of the dance floor must add up to 17. Good luck! Hint: Tables 9 and 12 are opposite each other.

NUMBERS UP!

This puzzle is as easy as 1, 2, 3. Fill in a number to complete each phrase. Some numbers are used more than once.

A bird in the hand is worth _____ in the bush.

On cloud _____

A stitch in time saves _____.

In _____ ear and out the other

Behind the _____ ball

_____ heads are better than _____.

A picture is worth _____ words.

Sail the _____ seas

Like _____ peas in a pod

_____-ring circus

_____ of _____ , a half dozen of the other

No _____ ways about it

Illustration: Jerry Zimmerman

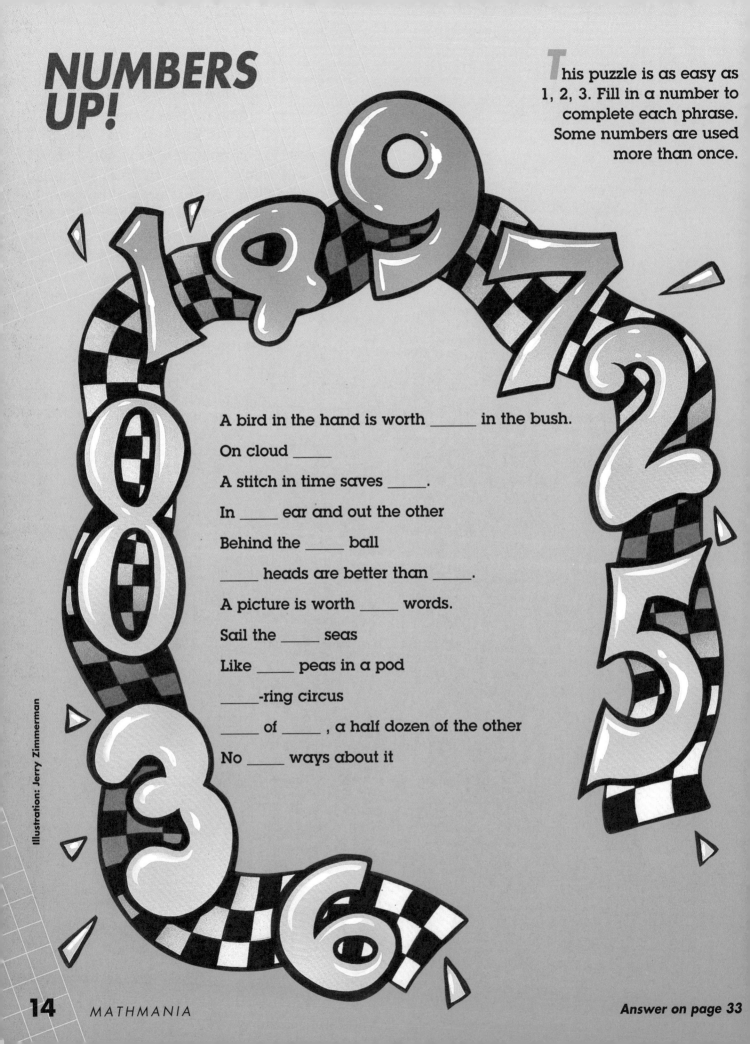

Answer on page 33

PRODUCE PROBLEM

FRUIT LIST
3 dozen oranges
$1\frac{1}{2}$ dozen pineapples
6 dozen apples
$7\frac{1}{2}$ dozen bananas
9 dozen pears

The Blue Butterfly Nature Club is selling baskets of fruit to raise money for its camping trip. Eli and Katie are in charge of dividing the food among 18 baskets. The contents of each basket must be the same. What must the two friends place in each one?

Hint on page 32

Answer on page 34

WHOSE HOME?

1. The Wallace family lives in a corner on top.
2. The O'Briens live in between the Gorman and Wallace families.
3. Dr. Rivera and his family live in the center.
4. Ms. Stevens and her boys are on the right.
5. The Barons live directly under the Stevens.
6. The Gormans are directly above Mr. Como.
7. The Garvey and Baron apartments are touching.
8. Mr. and Mrs. Perez took over Mr. Paige's first-floor home.
9. Mr. Como lives to the left of Dr. Rivera, as Phyllis faces the building.

Illustration: Lindy Burnett

Answer on page 34

17

WILT'S QUILT

The math club is making a quilt for the school auction. It is up to Wilt to finish the job. He must place symbols in the empty, solid squares. He can use > (greater than), < (less than) or = (equal to). Wilt has done a few, but you must help him finish the job. Remember that the open end of the symbol always points to the bigger number and the closed end to the smaller number. After you fill in the ones across, try to fill them in going up and down.

Hint on page 32

Illustration: Terry Kovalcik

Answer on page 34

HOCKEY HANDSHAKES

After the big hockey game, each of the Sharks shakes hands with each of the Panthers. If there are six players on each team, how many handshakes will there be altogether? Suppose the players shake their teammates' hands, too. How many handshakes would that add?

Illustration: Terry Kovalcik

Hint on page 32

Answer on page 34

TRAVEL TROUBLE

The two big suitcases look the same. How will Cary know which one is his? His passport is stamped in the order he visited six countries. Use that information to figure it out.

Illustration: Scott Peck

Answer on page 34

HOOP HEIGHTS

Here is the starting line-up for the Central School Rim Rockers. Can you give the height in feet and inches for each player?

Alice is 61 inches tall.
Judy and Chelsea are the same height.
Shelly is an inch taller than Chelsea.
Sue is between Alice and Shelly.
Judy is 3 inches shorter than Alice.

STARTING LINE-UP
Player Height

Alice _____

Judy _____

Chelsea _____

Shelly _____

Sue _____

Illustration: R. Michael Palan

Answer on page 34

CANDY COUNTER

Each piece of colorful candy costs less than 10 cents. Can you look at these prices and figure out the price of each kind?

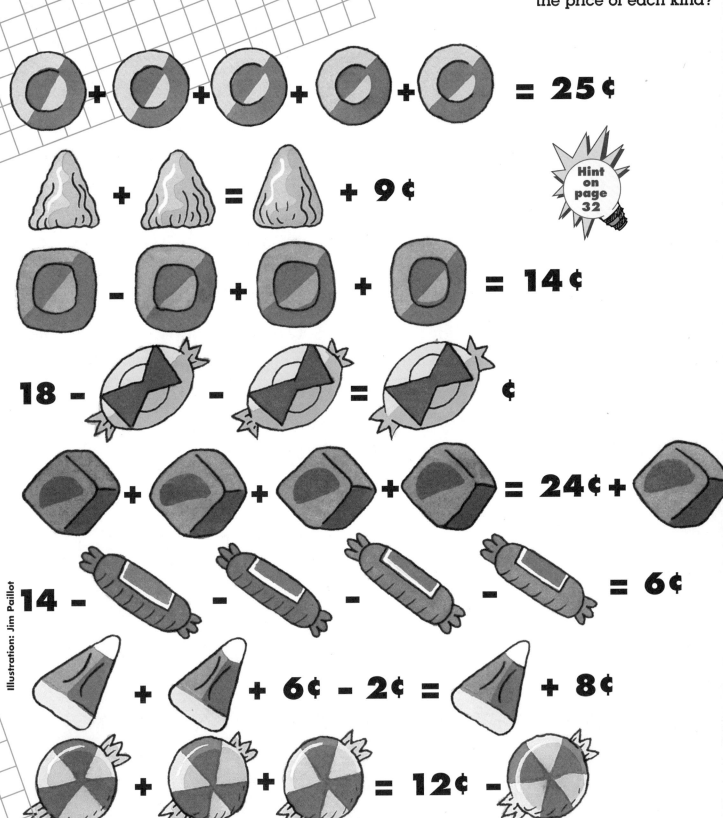

Hint on page 32

Illustration: Jim Paillot

Answer on page 34

GOING BANANAS

To solve this puzzle, first look at the pair of numbers under each space. Match the numbers to the bananas. Find the first number in the pair along the orange line, and the second number along the green column. Then find the banana where those two numbers meet. Write the letter on top of that banana in the space above the pair of numbers. Hint: The first letter is B. This is the letter on the banana where the orange 2 and the green 3 meet.

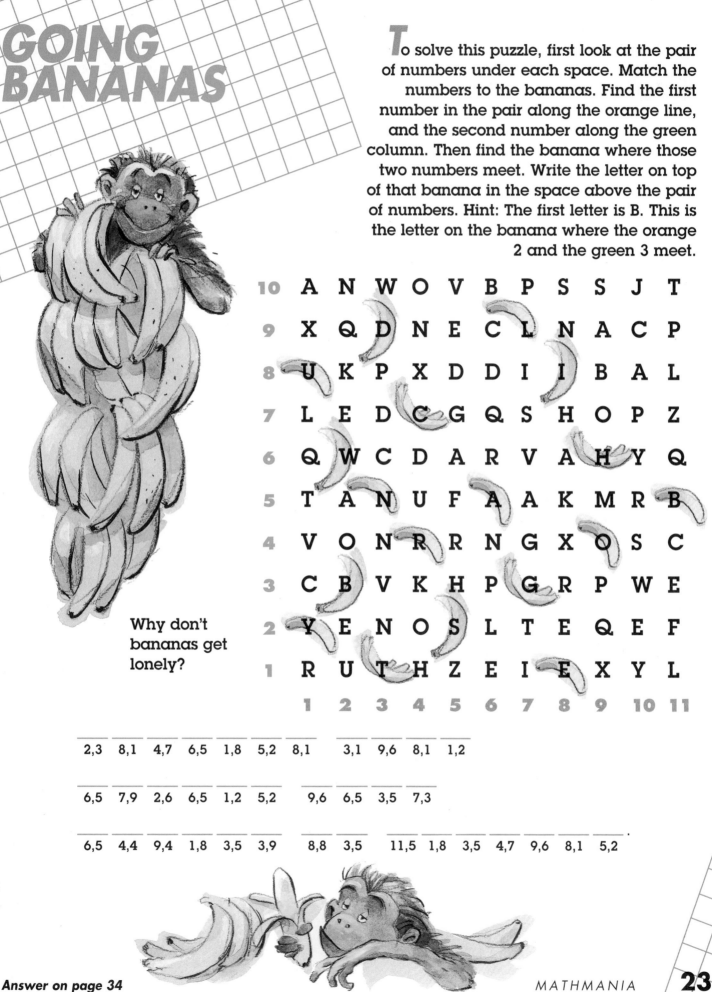

10	A	N	W	O	V	B	P	S	S	J	T
9	X	Q	D	N	E	C	L	N	A	C	P
8	U	K	P	X	D	D	I	I	B	A	L
7	L	E	D	C	G	Q	S	H	P	Z	
6	Q	W	C	D	A	R	V	A	H	Y	Q
5	T	A	N	U	F	A	A	K	M	R	B
4	V	O	N	R	R	N	G	X	O	S	C
3	C	B	V	K	H	P	G	R	P	W	E
2	Y	E	N	O	S	L	T	E	Q	E	F
1	R	U	T	H	Z	E	I	E	X	Y	L
	1	2	3	4	5	6	7	8	9	10	11

Why don't bananas get lonely?

___ ___ ___ ___ ___ ___ ___   ___ ___ ___ ___
2,3 8,1 4,7 6,5 1,8 5,2 8,1   3,1 9,6 8,1 1,2

___ ___ ___ ___ ___ ___   ___ ___ ___ ___
6,5 7,9 2,6 6,5 1,2 5,2   9,6 6,5 3,5 7,3

___ ___ ___ ___ ___ ___   ___ ___   ___ ___ ___ ___ ___ ___ ___ .
6,5 4,4 9,4 1,8 3,5 3,9   8,8 3,5   11,5 1,8 3,5 4,7 9,6 8,1 5,2

Answer on page 34

DIGIT DOES IT

A crime has been committed at Pauline's Pet Palace! Fortunately, Inspector Digit, world-famous detective, is on the job. Whoever broke in left a message floating in a bottle in the tropical fish tank. Help Inspector Digit crack the

Illustration: John Nez

24

code and solve the case. Each number stands for a letter of the alphabet. As you figure out some words, use them to figure out others. Hint: The first line reads "Dear Inspector Digit."

$\overline{1}\ \overline{8}\ \overline{12}\ \overline{7}$ $\overline{6}\ \overline{14}\ \overline{2}\ \overline{4}\ \overline{8}\ \overline{13}\ \overline{16}\ \overline{3}\ \overline{7}$ $\overline{1}\ \overline{6}\ \overline{20}\ \overline{6}\ \overline{16}$'

$\overline{6}\quad\overline{5}\ \overline{8}\ \overline{12}\ \overline{7}\ \overline{1}$ $\overline{16}\ \overline{5}\ \overline{8}\ \overline{7}\ \overline{8}$ $\overline{15}\ \overline{12}\ \overline{2}$

$\overline{20}\ \overline{3}\ \overline{22}\ \overline{1}$ $\overline{5}\ \overline{8}\ \overline{7}\ \overline{8}$, $\overline{9}\ \overline{10}\ \overline{16}$ $\overline{12}\ \overline{22}\ \overline{22}$ $\overline{6}$

$\overline{24}\ \overline{3}\ \overline{10}\ \overline{14}\ \overline{1}$ $\overline{15}\ \overline{8}\ \overline{7}\ \overline{8}$ $\overline{20}\ \overline{3}\ \overline{22}\ \overline{1}$ $\overline{24}\ \overline{6}\ \overline{2}\ \overline{5}$.

$\overline{6}\quad\overline{1}\ \overline{6}\ \overline{1}\ \overline{14}\ \overline{16}$ $\overline{16}\ \overline{12}\ \overline{11}\ \overline{8}$ $\overline{16}\ \overline{5}\ \overline{8}\ \overline{17}$'

$\overline{9}\ \overline{10}\ \overline{16}$ $\overline{6}\quad\overline{1}\ \overline{6}\ \overline{1}$ $\overline{11}\ \overline{14}\ \overline{3}\ \overline{13}\ \overline{11}$ $\overline{3}\ \overline{18}\ \overline{8}\ \overline{7}$ $\overline{12}$

$\overline{13}\ \overline{12}\ \overline{20}\ \overline{8}$ $\overline{24}\ \overline{10}\ \overline{22}\ \overline{22}$ $\overline{3}\ \overline{24}$ $\overline{4}\ \overline{8}\ \overline{16}\ \overline{17}\ \overline{6}\ \overline{13}\ \overline{8}$.

$\overline{2}\ \overline{6}\ \overline{19}\ \overline{16}\ \overline{8}\ \overline{8}\ \overline{14}$ $\overline{12}\ \overline{7}\ \overline{8}$ $\overline{22}\ \overline{3}\ \overline{3}\ \overline{2}\ \overline{8}$.

$\overline{13}\ \overline{12}\ \overline{14}$ $\overline{21}\ \overline{3}\ \overline{10}$ $\overline{24}\ \overline{6}\ \overline{14}\ \overline{1}$ $\overline{16}\ \overline{5}\ \overline{8}\ \overline{17}$?

$\overline{2}\ \overline{6}\ \overline{14}\ \overline{13}\ \overline{8}\ \overline{7}\ \overline{8}\ \overline{22}\ \overline{21}$,

$\overline{24}\ \overline{7}\ \overline{8}\ \overline{1}\ \overline{12}$ $\overline{17}\ \overline{6}\ \overline{13}\ \overline{8}$

Answer on page 34

TWO STEPS

START

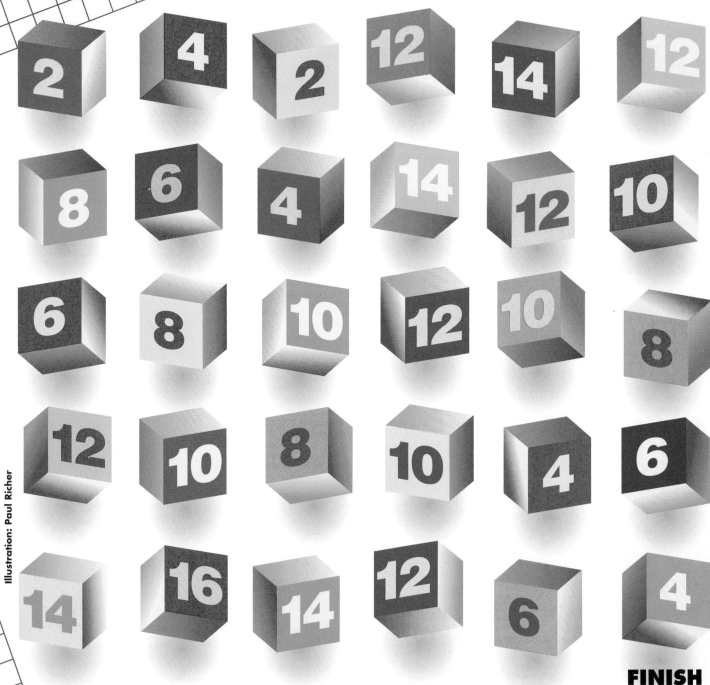

Illustration: Paul Richer

FINISH

Answer on page 35

A MATTER OF DEGREES

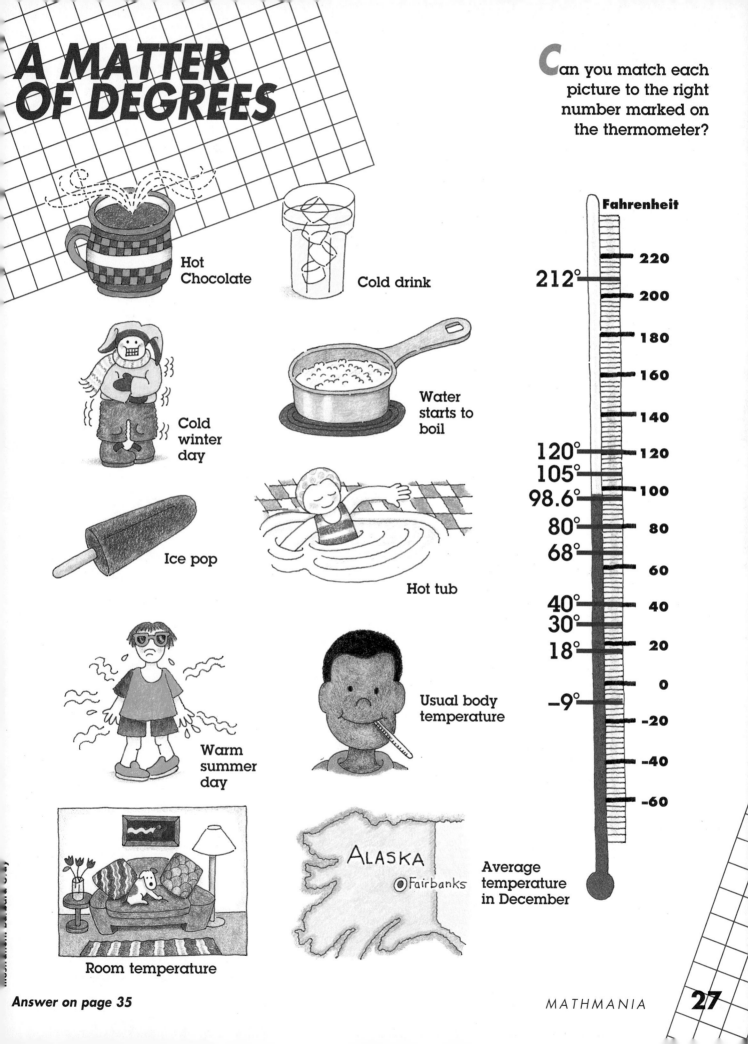

Hot Chocolate

Cold drink

Cold winter day

Water starts to boil

Ice pop

Hot tub

Warm summer day

Usual body temperature

Room temperature

ALASKA
Fairbanks

Average temperature in December

Fahrenheit

212°
120°
105°
98.6°
80°
68°
40°
30°
18°
−9°

220
200
180
160
140
120
100
80
60
40
20
0
−20
−40
−60

BEAUCOUP BOUQUETS

A sweet-smelling shipment has arrived at Blossom's Flower Shop. Two bouquets have already been put in vases. It is up to you to help Blossom arrange the rest. Here is the trick. The total

Illustration: Jerry Zimmerman

Hint on page 32

Answer on page 35

number of flowers across, down, and diagonally must add up to 21. Keep the bunches together. Write the number of flowers that must go into each of the vases on Blossom's shelves.

SCRAMBLED PICTURE

Copy these mixed-up rectangles into the spaces on the next page to put together a "cool customer."

A-4   A-2   A-1   A-3

B-3   B-1   B-4   B-2

C-4   C-3   C-2   C-1

D-1   D-2   D-4   D-3

Illustration: Rob Sepanek

Answer on page 35

The letters and numbers tell
you where each square
belongs. The first one, A-3,
has been done for you.

	1	2	3	4
A				
B				
C				
D				

HINTS AND BRIGHT IDEAS

*T*hese hints will help with some of the trickier puzzles.

TILE TOTALS (pages 4–5)

You can count up the tiles on each patio one by one. But you can also count one complete row and one complete column and multiply to get your answer. For instance, the first patio uses 5 × 4 = 20 tiles.

PIG GIGGLE (pages 8–9)

The shape for the letter *S* is made from the top corner. The numbers 35 and 85 are in the shape. Since 35 + 85 = 120, write S in space 120. Can you keep going now?

FRUZZLE PUZZLE (page 11)

Each Fruzzle must have a triangle shape in its body. If you can figure out the other two things, you can find the Fruzzles in the puzzle.

PRODUCE PROBLEM (page 15)

First figure out the exact number of fruits of each kind. Then divide the number for each fruit by the number of baskets to get your answer.

WILT'S QUILT (page 18)

Look at the top row on the right. You will see 75 ☐ 50. Since 75 is the bigger number, you would write 75 > 50.

HOCKEY HANDSHAKES (page 19)

To answer the first part of the question, think about it this way: Each Shark will shake 6 Panther hands. Can you figure it out now? And remember, when shaking with your own team, don't count yourself.

CANDY COUNTER (page 22)

Here is another way to look at the first one. There are 5 circle candies that cost a total of 25 cents. Another way to say this is 5 × ? = 25. What number times 5 equals 25?

BEAUCOUP BOUQUETS (pages 28–29)

First count the number of flowers in each bouquet and write the numbers next to them. Working with numbers instead of flowers may help you figure it out.

ANSWERS

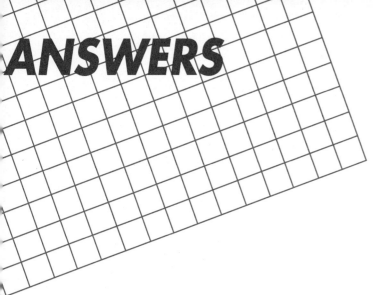

COVER
The hands of the clock should be placed so that the 1, 2, 3, 10, 11, 12 are on one side. On the other side are 4, 5, 6, 7, 8, and 9. The sum of each side is 39.

DINO RIDDLE (page 3)
A STEGO-SNORE-US

TILE TOTALS (pages 4–5)
1. $5 \times 4 = 20$
2. $3 \times 5 = 15$
3. $5 \times 8 = 40$
4. $4 \times 10 = 40$
5. $4 \times 7 = 28$

Dan will need 143 tiles in all.

NUMBER NEWS (page 6)
The stories about the heat wave, the crowd at the ball game, the space mission, and the sunken treasure are using estimates. The ones about the triplets, the 100th birthday, and the Blue Sox are exact figures.

FOLLOW THE FLAKES (page 7)
Here is our answer. You may have found another.

PIG GIGGLE (pages 8–9)
Let's be pen pals.

TRIANGLE TRAP (page 10)
We counted at least 59 triangles. How many did you find?

FRUZZLE PUZZLE (page 11)

D, G, and K are fruzzles. Fruzzles must be green, have a single triangle shape inside, and 3 antennae.

TRIPLE PLAY (page 12)

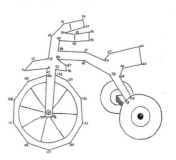

TABLE TROUBLE (page 13)

NUMBERS UP! (page 14)
A bird in the hand is worth 2 in the bush.
On cloud 9
A stitch in time saves 9.
In 1 ear and out the other
Behind the 8 ball
2 heads are better than 1.
A picture is worth 1,000 words.
Sail the 7 seas
Like 2 peas in a pod
3-ring circus
6 of 1, a half dozen of the other
No 2 ways about it

PRODUCE PROBLEM (page 15)

Each basket contains 18 items: 2 oranges, 1 pineapple, 4 apples, 5 bananas, and 6 pears.

WHOSE HOME? (pages 16-17)

WILT'S QUILT (page 18)

HOCKEY HANDSHAKES (page 19)

Since each Shark shakes six hands, the answer is 6 × 6, or 36.

If they shook their teammates' hands, the Sharks would add 5 + 4 + 3 + 2 + 1 = 15 extra handshakes. The Panthers would also have 15 extras, so there would be 30 more handshakes. The new total would be 36 + 30 = 66 handshakes.

TRAVEL TROUBLE (page 20)

HOOP HEIGHTS (page 21)

Alice: 5'1"
Judy: 4'10"
Chelsea: 4'10"
Shelly: 4'11"
Sue: 5'0"

CANDY COUNTER (page 22)

5 + 5 + 5 + 5 + 5 = 25
9 + 9 = 9 + 9
7 − 7 + 7 + 7 = 14
18 − 6 − 6 = 6
8 + 8 + 8 + 8 = 24 + 8
14 − 2 − 2 − 2 − 2 = 6
4 + 4 + 6 − 2 = 4 + 8
3 + 3 + 3 = 12 − 3

GOING BANANAS (page 23)

Why don't bananas get lonely?
Because they always hang around in bunches.

DIGIT DOES IT (pages 24-25)

Dear Inspector Digit,
I heard there was gold here, but all I found were goldfish. I didn't take them, but I did knock over a cage full of pet mice. Sixteen are loose. Can you find them?
Sincerely,
Freda Mice